MEDIEVAL LEGO®

GREYSON BEIGHTS

No Starch Press
San Francisco

Printed in China

First printing

19 18 17 16 15   1 2 3 4 5 6 7 8 9

ISBN-10: 1-59327-650-8
ISBN-13: 978-1-59327-650-8

Publisher: William Pollock
Production Editor: Alison Law
Cover and Interior Design: Beth Middleworth
Cover Models: Elliott Feldman and Günther Möbius
Developmental Editor: Tyler Ortman
Copyeditor: Rachel Monaghan
Compositor: Alison Law
Proofreader: Paula L. Fleming

For information on distribution, translations, or bulk sales,
please contact No Starch Press, Inc. directly:

No Starch Press, Inc.
245 8th Street, San Francisco, CA 94103
phone: 415.863.9900; info@nostarch.com; www.nostarch.com

Library of Congress Cataloging-in-Publication Data

Beights, Greyson.
Medieval LEGO / by Greyson Beights.
pages cm
Summary: "An illustrated history of Medieval England from 1028 to 1485, using scenes created in LEGO. Features commentary by medieval history professors about notable events and figures"-- Provided by publisher.
ISBN 978-1-59327-650-8 -- ISBN 1-59327-650-8
1. Great Britain--History--1066-1687. 2. LEGO toys. I. Title.
DA176.B43 2015
942.02--dc23
2015014401

Production Date: 5/29/2015
Plant & Location: Printed by Everbest Printing (Guangzhou, China), Co. Ltd
Job / Batch #: 54148-0 / EPC 707070

For my parents, Angela and Gaylon,

who provided me with

the opportunity, resources, support,

and motivation

to accomplish my dreams

A NOTE OF THANKS

First and foremost, I would like to thank God for giving me strength, wisdom, and curiosity. Thank you to my parents, Angela and Gaylon, for their endless love and support. Thank you to my grandparents, Georgia and Larry, for making my LEGO collection what it is today and for always being there. Thank you to my sister, Lauren, for keeping the journey fun. To my brothers, Roland and York, thank you for all the amusement. I also would especially like to thank all the contributors. Without them, this book would not have been possible. Their endless passion for the subject is awe inspiring. Lastly, I would like to thank my editors, Alison Law and Tyler Ortman, for giving me the truly distinct honor of working with them. I could not have asked for better support, help, and guidance throughout the whole process—from start to finish.

• PREFACE •

It is essential that we learn history. History tells us where we've been and where we might yet go. Winston Churchill once stated, "The farther back you can look, the farther forward you are likely to see."

The medieval period was a time of great adventure and excitement—of kings, queens, knights, castles, and great wars. But it was a time of great hardships as well—of servitude, famines, and plagues.

To present this great historical period, I enlisted the help of expert scholars and LEGO builders from around the world. This book narrates the history of medieval England using short passages and LEGO scenes. I hope you find it an entertaining and educational read. I believe that after reading this book, you'll agree with me that the medieval period in England was one of the most exciting in history.

• CONTENTS •

PART III: 1346-1485

PART I: 1028–1214

WILLIAM THE CONQUEROR

1028-1087

In 1066, William the Duke of Normandy (a large region in northern France) planned and carried out one of the most amazing military operations of the medieval period. His invasion of Anglo-Saxon England, known as the Norman Conquest, would totally change the course of English history.

When childless English king Edward the Confessor died without a direct heir, three rivals wanted the crown, including William. When the Anglo-Saxon nobles chose one of their own, Earl Harold Godwinson, as the next king, William decided to invade England and take the throne by force. He spent months putting together an army; building a fleet; and gathering horses, weapons, and supplies. Crossing the English Channel in September, William defeated Harold at the Battle of Hastings on October 14.

After capturing several important towns, including London, he was crowned King William on Christmas Day. Although he faced several rebellions in the following years, he eventually secured the rest of England, in part by building many castles throughout the country.

By the end of his reign, William had replaced the old Anglo-Saxon ruling class with a new, French-speaking Norman monarchy and nobility. As a result, England was

drawn into French politics and was greatly influenced by French culture, a situation that would continue throughout the rest of the medieval period.

Because of his many military victories, William was named William the Conqueror.

—DR. GILBERT BOGNER

BATTLE OF HASTINGS

1066

The Battle of Hastings was the beginning of William's invasion of England. On September 28, 1066, William landed in England and drew Harold Godwinson, the current king of England, into a battle that would decide who would be king.

When Harold heard that William had landed, he hurried south toward Hastings from Stamford Bridge, where he had defeated an invading Viking army. William learned of Harold's approach on October 13.

The next morning at dawn, William and his Norman army moved toward Harold's Saxon army. William found that Harold held a strong position at the top of a ridge.

Both armies had thousands of men and were closely matched. Harold's army fought on foot using battle axes and swords, while William led a force of infantry, archers, and cavalry.

William attacked first. The attack failed, and a panic spread through his army with false rumors of William's death. But William showed he was alive and rallied his troops once again.

The battle lasted the rest of the day. The Normans launched several attacks and drew their opponents from the hill by staging phony retreats, but the Saxons stood their ground—worn down but not defeated.

William needed to win or his invasion would fail. At last, one final attack by William's army broke through the Saxons, and Harold was cut down under his dragon flag.

—DR. STEPHEN MORILLO

SIEGE OF JERUSALEM

1099

On June 7, 1099, the army of the First Crusade camped outside its goal, the City of Jerusalem. The pope had called for the war to recapture Christianity's holy city and free Christians in the region from Muslim rule.

The Crusader army, which included William the Conqueror's son Robert Curthose, had been marching since 1096 to regain the Holy Lands. Although it had set out with 60,000 men, the army was reduced to 1,200 knights and 12,000 foot by previous battles, disease, and fatigue.

The army was too small to surround Jerusalem completely. Because the east and west sides of the city were guarded by steep slopes, the Crusaders chose to attack only the north and south walls.

The Crusaders knew that the Egyptian rulers of the city were raising an army to attack them, and the Crusaders had only one ladder. In spite of these issues, they assaulted the city by scaling its walls on June 13—but failed.

Cleverly, Robert Curthose and the Crusaders then built four-story siege towers on wheels to roll up against the city walls on the north and south sides. On the night of July 9, they surprised Jerusalem's defenders by moving the northern siege tower from the west end of the north wall to a weak spot on the east. Their assault began in earnest on July 13.

Duke Godfrey de Bouillon, who later ruled the city, sat on top of the northern siege tower firing his crossbow. The southern siege tower was set aflame by the defenders, but Godfrey's men pushed their tower up to the wall and broke into the city. The army exalting,

THE CRUSADERS BREACH THE WALLS

with their blood up, massacred the people living in the city and rushed to worship at the Church of the Holy Sepulchre. This victory led to the creation of the Kingdom of Jerusalem.

—PROFESSOR JOHN FRANCE

A HUNTING PARTY

DEATH OF WILLIAM RUFUS

1100

Medieval kings loved to hunt, but it could be a dangerous adventure.

Under Forest Law, the Norman kings created large areas of forest for their own private hunting grounds. Commoners were not allowed in these green woods. The punishment for trespassing or poaching the king's deer was steep—losing a hand, being blinded, or even being put to death.

The largest of these forests was the New Forest, created by William the Conqueror. To make it, many villages and farmsteads were destroyed, and the people who lived there left without homes.

In 1100, William's son William Rufus, the second Norman king, was hunting in the New Forest when an arrow shot by one of his friends, Walter Tyrell, missed the deer he was aiming at and hit the king. William Rufus died at once. Tyrell fled, and William's corpse was carried to the nearby city of Winchester for burial.

William Rufus's younger brother, Henry, quickly seized the royal treasure and crowned himself king. Was this a plot with Tyrell as the assassin? We will never know.

Strangely enough, this was the second of William the Conqueror's sons to die in the New Forest. His son Richard of Normandy had died in an accident in the New Forest in 1081. Some people thought these royal deaths were a just punishment for creating the New Forest and driving out its residents.

—PROFESSOR ROBERT BARTLETT

WILLIAM RUFUS SHOT BY AN ARROW

ELEANOR OF AQUITAINE

1122-1204

One of the most powerful women in all of medieval history, Eleanor of Aquitaine held the balance between English and French royal power.

As a child, Eleanor inherited Aquitaine, a large region in the southwestern corner of modern-day France. When she married the French king, Louis VII, Aquitaine became one of his territories, making the area he ruled much larger. (Before their marriage, he ruled only a small part of what is now France.)

But Louis was more in love with her than she was with him, and their marriage became troubled.

Eventually, their marriage ended, and the reason given was that they were too closely related to be legally married. But this was probably just an excuse, as Eleanor soon married the future King Henry II of England, to whom she was also closely related.

This marriage had huge effects on England and France because it united Aquitaine with Henry's lands, which would soon include England as well as large areas in France. Eleanor's marriage to Henry became troubled as well, and she and her sons led a rebellion against her husband. After an 18-month struggle, they lost and she was put in prison for 16 years, until her husband's death. Then, at age 67, she was released. Two of her sons, Richard the Lionheart and John, succeeded her husband to the throne.

The year of Eleanor's death, the English crown lost many of its French lands, but not Aquitaine. It remained united with England until the mid-15th century.

—PROFESSOR DAVID D'AVRAY

BATTLE OF THE STANDARD

1138

In 1135, Stephen became king of England after his uncle King Henry I died. By doing so, he kept Henry's daughter and heir, Matilda, from taking the throne.

People immediately began to argue about whether he was the rightful king. The suspicious circumstances under which he became king meant that by 1138, anyone unhappy with Stephen could look to Matilda as a replacement.

And so, revolts and invasions broke out across Normandy and England.

Matilda's uncle, King David of Scotland, invaded England from the north. King Stephen was busy fighting rebel barons in the south, so the local people tried to defend the area against the Scottish.

In the king's absence, Archbishop Thurstan of York had enough clout to pull together the northern barons and local priests and their followers to help protect the land. The impromptu army created a colorful standard—a mast with three saints' flags and a container of Communion host. Mounted on a cart and used as the army's command post, the one-of-a-kind standard gave the battle name.

THE LAST SCOTTISH ATTACK

Near Northallerton, the forces of the archbishop and King David met. The English army won by standing its ground against repeated Scottish attacks. The first attack came from supposedly naked berserkers from Glasgow, the next from the Scottish cavalry, and the final one from the Scottish infantry. All failed. The outnumbered English were able to turn the tables and chase the retreating enemy.

Although David's forces lost the battle, Stephen later granted many of his demands so the English people could have peace on the Scottish border.

—DR. STEVEN ISAAC

RICHARD THE LIONHEART ARRIVING AT THE HOLY LAND WITH HIS ARMY

SIEGE OF ACRE

1189-1191

Acre, now a port town in modern-day Israel, was once under the control of the Crusaders, but it was lost to the Muslim leader Saladin in 1187, after the Battle of Hattin. Saladin's forces then pushed through other Crusader-held towns and cities, reversing the Crusaders' success. Only the cities of Antioch, Tripoli, and Tyre held out against Saladin's attacks.

On August 28, 1189, King Guy of Jerusalem tried to invade Acre to restore his reputation and recapture the town from Saladin.

This siege was a draw; neither side won or lost. Saladin's army surrounded the Crusaders' camp, and conditions in the camp quickly became miserable. The Crusaders' only hope was Frederick of Germany, the Holy Roman Emperor, who they heard would soon arrive to help them. But he died on June 10, 1190, and his army was destroyed by plague. Enough fresh Crusaders arrived from Europe to keep the siege going, but all hope of success now depended on the kings of England and France.

King Philip of France arrived in April 1191, and Richard the Lionheart of England came in June. Although these two did not trust each other, their giant catapults and fresh troops forced Saladin to surrender the city

THE THREE KINGS: PHILIP OF FRANCE, GUY OF JERUSALEM, AND RICHARD THE LIONHEART

by July 12. The lives of Saladin's soldiers in the city would have been spared in return for a ransom. But Saladin failed to pay. As a result, 2,700 of his men were executed in revenge for the disaster at Hattin and the hardships of the siege.

—PROFESSOR JOHN FRANCE

BLONDEL SEARCHES FOR RICHARD THE LIONHEART

THE CAPTIVITY OF RICHARD THE LIONHEART

Richard I of England, nicknamed "the Lionheart," was a famous warrior king and a leader of the Christian crusade in the Holy Land.

His greatest enemy on the battlefield was the Muslim leader Saladin. But Richard quarreled with other Christian leaders as well, including Duke Leopold V of Austria, who felt Richard had insulted him.

Unfortunately for Richard, as he was returning by sea from his wars in the Holy Land, his ship was wrecked and he had to pass through the duke of Austria's lands. He tried to travel in disguise, but because of his lavish spending, people became suspicious about who he was.

While in Vienna, Richard fell into the hands of his enemy, the duke, and was put in prison in a mountain castle far from the city. Legend tells of how Richard's loyal minstrel Blondel went from castle to castle searching for his master. He would sing the first line of a song they both knew and wait for a reply. One day, from a window in one of the castles, he heard the king's voice singing the next line.

Richard spent more than a year as a prisoner until a huge ransom—34 tons of silver—was paid for his release in 1194. His mother, Eleanor of Aquitaine, helped to raise the funds. After his release, he continued his life as a warrior and king until, five years later, he died from a crossbow wound.

—PROFESSOR ROBERT BARTLETT

EXCOMMUNICATION OF KING JOHN

1209

In 1205, the important job of archbishop of Canterbury became available. For many years, this caused a serious conflict between the king of England and the pope.

King John disagreed with the monks of Canterbury about whom to choose. Pope Innocent III didn't like the choices of either the king or the monks, so he made his own choice for the job, a man named Stephen Langton.

KING JOHN UPON HEARING THE NEWS OF HIS EXCOMMUNICATION

John was very angry at the pope for meddling in English affairs. He refused to let Langton come to England and wouldn't recognize him as archbishop. The pope responded by placing all of England under an interdict, a special kind of punishment.

During the interdict, no Christian church services could take place, and the dead could not be buried in holy ground. Some say that coffins were hung from trees to protect them from animals while people waited for the interdict to be lifted. Even the church bells were silent.

After five years under the interdict, John still refused to change his mind, so the pope decided to excommunicate the king. Excommunication meant John

LANGTON RETURNS TO ENGLAND

couldn't take part in Christian worship. Other Christians weren't supposed to support him or even talk to him. The dramatic excommunication ceremony probably involved blowing out candles and ringing a special bell to show that the king was a spiritual outcast.

Even some of John's people decided to rise up against him. According to the pope, lesser lords had no obligation to follow their oath to obey John. The barons even invited the French king to invade England. When he realized how bad the situation was, John gave in. He allowed Langton to return to England and recognized him as archbishop. But unfortunately for King John, his troubles would not end there.

—DR. KATHLEEN NEAL

THE FOUNDING OF THE UNIVERSITY OF OXFORD

1214

One of the most important inventions of the Middle Ages was the university—a place of higher education for young men who would go on to work for the church and state. (No women were admitted in those times.) The idea of a university was not created in one single moment but grew gradually.

In England, the town of Oxford had a reputation as a center of study by the 1180s and 1190s. Even then, the town was full of teachers and students who studied the arts, law, and theology.

The University of Oxford, as an official organization, developed because of a dramatic clash between students and townsfolk in 1209. A student had murdered a local woman, and when the townsmen could not find him, rioters hanged his three roommates instead. In outrage, the teachers and students left Oxford, some of them to establish a new place of study at Cambridge.

The remaining teachers and students did not return until 1214, when a high-ranking church official drew up an agreement: the townsmen of Oxford had to agree to charge the students a lower rent, provide funds for poor students, and sell food and drink at a fair price. This new arrangement was to be headed by an official called a chancellor. The oldest university in the English-speaking world had now taken shape.

—PROFESSOR ROBERT BARTLETT

ROBIN HOOD

c. 1200

Robin Hood's story was first told in late medieval ballads and plays. In these early sources, recorded from about 1400 onward, his name is spelled *Robyn Hode*. According to folklore, he and his "merry band" of men enjoyed life in the summers in Sherwood Forest, among other real-life English locations.

They harried and took money from the bullying sheriff of Nottingham and corrupt monks. But they were faithful to the social and religious systems led by the king and St. Mary. Depending on the source, Robin's king could have been Edward I, Edward II, Edward III, or Richard the Lionheart! This folk story has had a remarkably long life.

Although Robin Hood's men fought well with swords and wooden staffs, their favored weapon was the powerful longbow. Robin was the best archer among them.

His fame has lasted for centuries, and his story has appeared in countless films and novels. He is a hero who stands for doing what's right, giving generously to the poor, and fighting against oppression of all kinds.

—PROFESSOR STEPHEN KNIGHT

PART II: 1215–1345

SIGNING OF MAGNA CARTA

1215

Magna Carta means *Great Charter*. In other words, it's the Latin way to say a big legal document. It's very famous now, but details about the moment it came into being are uncertain.

Magna Carta records the result of talks between King John and a group of important barons and bishops who were unhappy with how he ruled England. They were so angry with his bad policies and heavy taxes that they had sworn not to obey him anymore.

To prevent the argument from turning into a war, the king agreed to make some special promises. There were long talks about what these would be. Many people took part, including the archbishop of Canterbury and the most senior nobles of England. Both sides probably also had teams of lawyers and advisors.

In the summer of 1215, when the final draft was ready, the king's personal seal was put on the document to show his approval. Copies were made and sent all over the kingdom to let people know what the king had pledged. Some of these points seem strange today, like the promise to remove all the fish traps from the River Thames. The promises were mainly for the rich and powerful; they didn't apply to people lower in society. Most related to money and the legal rights of the displeased barons and nobles.

But King John's promises could not be trusted. As soon as Magna Carta was written, he asked the pope to overrule it. He said that he had been forced into approving it. The pope agreed, and the promises became invalid. It wasn't until after King John's death that Magna Carta came to life once more.

—DR. KATHLEEN NEAL

MATTHEW PARIS

1200-1259

Matthew Paris was a monk at St Albans, a rich monastery near London. He wrote a history of England during the 13th century and made his views of kings and their actions very clear. His accounts are important for our knowledge of this period.

Matthew Paris was also a political commentator. Because Matthew wrote after King John's death, he was able to be very critical of John.

ST ALBANS ABBEY

He included in his chronicle an account of the troubles that led to the signing of Magna Carta. He even added a poem that claimed that King John had gone to Hell, and when he arrived, he had made Hell *worse*.

The monk also made maps of Britain and of the pilgrims' route to Jerusalem. Using his skill as an artist, he recorded the miracles of saints and unusual sights, such as an elephant in a royal exhibit.

Because of his religious devotion and political skills, he was sent on an embassy to Norway. He was also interested in finding ways to predict the future. He left illustrated accounts of both subjects, as well as his chronicles and dramatic stories about saints, including the murder of Thomas Becket.

—DR. ANNE LAWRENCE-MATHERS

ROGER BACON

1214-1292

Roger Bacon was an important early scholar. We don't know exactly when or where he was born, but he was an active writer and teacher in the second half of the 13th century. By 1267, Bacon completed three major works: the *Bigger Book* (*Opus Majus*), the *Littler Book* (*Opus Minus*), and the *Third Book* (*Opus Tertium*). He wrote about philosophy, but his main interest was in understanding the world around him.

Much like a modern scientist, Bacon argued that one could better understand how the physical world worked through careful observation and record keeping.

He explored the science of vision (mirrors, lenses, how the eye works), how mathematics can explain the physical world, and astronomy.

Roger Bacon was an extraordinary medieval thinker. Although he was not a modern scientist, he understood things about the natural world that had previously been utterly mysterious to his contemporaries.

—PROFESSOR JOHN ARNOLD

ROGER BACON IN HIS WORKSHOP

ENGLISH RULE ARRIVES IN NORTHUMBERLAND

TREATY OF YORK

1237

The kingdoms of England and Scotland took shape slowly. By the year 1000, they had certainly come into existence, but their exact boundaries were not clear. For several hundred years, the kings of England and the kings of Scotland tried to extend their power at the expense of their neighbor when they could.

Warfare was not constant. But strong kings like David I of Scotland took the chance to control territory deep into what is now England, and formidable English rulers like Henry II pushed the frontier back again.

The Treaty of York in 1237 was intended to settle the matter. Henry III of England and Alexander II of Scotland met at York. Alexander agreed that the northern counties of Northumberland, Cumberland, and Westmorland would belong to the king of England. In return, Alexander received rich estates in England.

This was not the end of wars between Scotland and England (indeed, quite far from it!). But the frontier established by the Treaty of York is, more or less, the same today.

—PROFESSOR ROBERT BARTLETT

ALEXANDER II AND HENRY III MAKE A PACT

THE ENGLISH PARLIAMENT
CONFRONTS THE KING

FIRST ENGLISH PARLIAMENT

1265

A group of barons led by Simon de Montfort had taken control of England and captured King Henry III in battle. The baron rebels wanted to force Henry to keep some important promises made by his father, King John, like the ones written in Magna Carta.

One important demand was for the king to meet with representatives of the people and take their advice. So, in 1265, the barons decided to hold a parliament.

English kings had held big meetings called *parliaments* before, but these meetings had involved only the most powerful noblemen. This time the rebels invited not just the barons but also knights from all the shires of England. These people would represent the entire *community of the realm*—in other words, all the king's subjects, not just the powerful ones. This was a big step. Kings had never been forced to take notice of so many people's opinions before.

The parliament met in Westminster, then a village near London, to talk about how England should be ruled. King Henry III, who was still a prisoner, had to sit quietly and listen.

Montfort wanted representatives from all over England to make it look like his rebellion had lots of support, which he needed because keeping Henry prisoner made him look bad. In fact, some thought Montfort just wanted power for himself. Others thought it was wrong for him to put himself above the king. Several people who had been invited didn't attend the parliament, to avoid supporting him.

Soon after, Montfort was defeated in battle and killed. However, his idea of having a parliament to represent everyone had a big effect on how the English Parliament developed later.

—DR. KATHLEEN NEAL

WILLIAM WALLACE

1270-1305

In 1286, King Alexander III of Scotland died, leaving no clear heir to the throne. Thirteen different people thought they should be the next ruler of Scotland! King Edward I of England was asked to help sort it out. He decided that a man named John Balliol should become king. But when Edward later demanded that the Scottish lords fight on his side against France (England was at war with France), they refused. Instead, the lords and Balliol made a treaty with France.

WILLIAM WALLACE AT STERLING BRIDGE

This led to a war between Scotland and England, which England quickly won in 1296. King Edward removed Balliol from the throne and ruled the country directly. This decision was not accepted by many Scottish people. In 1297, the younger son of a Scottish knight, William Wallace, led a popular uprising.

Wallace's army defeated an English army at Stirling Bridge, prompting Edward to lead a much bigger army north to fight them. More skirmishes and battles took place over the next few years. The English won some of the battles—notably at Falkirk in 1298, even though many of the Welshmen in the English army refused to fight against the Scottish. But there was no decisive victory.

In 1303, Robert the Bruce, another claimant to the Scottish throne, joined forces with Edward to bring stability to Scotland. Wallace's rebels continued to resist, but most of the Scottish lords made peace with the English crown in 1304. A year later William Wallace was captured.

The English took Wallace south to London for trial and executed him cruelly—a horrible warning to any future rebels.

WILLIAM WALLACE

Robert the Bruce was eventually crowned king of Scotland by his supporters in 1306. He then led a fresh revolt against King Edward I and English rule.

—PROFESSOR JOHN ARNOLD

BATTLE OF FALKIRK

At Stirling Bridge, William Wallace earned a reputation as a guerilla fighter, using stealth and surprise tactics. But could he win in a traditional pitched battle on an open field?

At the Battle of Falkirk, Wallace faced a much larger opposing army, this time led by the English king himself, Edward I. Wallace organized his infantry into schiltroms, large circular shapes with two ranks of spearmen.

A "HEDGEHOG" FORMATION, OR SCHILTROM

The men in front knelt down and braced their 12-foot spears (called pikes) in the ground, slanted upward. The second row held their spears above the heads of those in front. The entire formation looked like a massive hedgehog, ready to stick the enemy if it charged. Behind the schiltroms, Wallace's cavalry waited to attack once the English broke ranks.

Before the battle, Wallace addressed his men: "I have brought you to the ring; dance the best you can."

Edward's knights, seeing nothing but open field between them and the schiltroms, charged on horseback. They did not realize that Wallace had placed the schiltroms behind marshy land. When the knights attacked, their horses got bogged down in the marsh, and the schiltroms held fast. The Scottish pikemen killed many of the English knights.

It looked like victory for Wallace, but the battle was not over. The remaining English knights withdrew and regrouped. Wallace's horsemen, behind the schiltroms, suddenly retreated from the battlefield, never having fought! Edward then deployed his archers, who used a relatively new weapon, the longbow. They loosed a hail of arrows on the trapped schiltroms, defeating them where mounted knights could not.

Wallace, having lost, barely escaped with his life.

—PROFESSOR PHILLIP C. ADAMO

AN ARCHER WITH A LONGBOW

FIRST ENGLISH PRINCE OF WALES

1301

When the Romans withdrew their legions from southern Britain in 410, the formerly united native Celtic Britons soon split back into quarrelsome local chiefdoms.

These divided peoples were unable to resist a new wave of invasions by the Germanic Angles and Saxons, who established what came to be called E*ngland*.

THE FIRST ENGLISH PRINCE OF WALES

The Angles and Saxons forced the native Britons into the western highlands, especially the mountainous central region the invaders called *Wales*.

Celtic Wales survived in this divided state until 1258, when it was finally united under the Prince of Gwynedd, Llywellyn ap Gruffydd. Taking the title Prince of Wales, he ruled the new principality until his death in 1282.

But his son and successor, Prince David, made the mistake of resisting the claims to overlordship by King Edward I of England, his more powerful neighbor. Edward deposed David and executed him for treason. Then he placed Wales under England's direct rule.

To retain control of Wales without abolishing the Celtic principality, Edward revived the title of Prince of Wales in February 1301. He then awarded the title and a reduced form of the principality to his only surviving son, the 16-year-old Edward of Caernarvon, who became King Edward II of England in 1307.

Edward II was deposed in 1327 without having conferred the principality on his own elder son, Edward of Windsor, who succeeded him as King Edward III. Edward III granted the principality to his eldest son, Edward of Woodstock, later known as "the Black Prince." From 1343 on, all English monarchs would grant Wales to their heir apparent (if they had one) when he came of age.

—PROFESSOR D'ARCY JONATHAN DACRE BOULTON

THE GREAT FAMINE

1315-1317

Between the years 1000 and 1300, the climate in medieval Europe became notably warmer. In fact, it was warm enough to grow grapes in southern England.

Because of this warm climate, more land was used for farming, more food was grown, and more people were born.

Medieval towns and cities grew larger as well. The city of London grew about ten times larger during the 12th and 13th centuries.

But early in the 14th century, the warmer climate ended. Europe and England had terrible storms and harsher winter weather. The harvests failed several years in a row, and livestock were affected by widespread disease. Of course, there was also political turmoil and warfare, which prevented communities from planning ahead or storing grain.

As a result, millions of people starved to death. The suffering across Europe was considerable.

By the end of the 14th century, the population of medieval England was much lower than at the beginning. Many people died from the Black Death, but a part of the population loss was caused earlier by the Great Famine.

—PROFESSOR JOHN ARNOLD

ROBERT THE BRUCE LOOKS OVER THE TREATY OF EDINBURGH-NORTHAMPTON

TREATY OF EDINBURGH-NORTHAMPTON

1328

Although English kings had claimed overlordship of Scotland since before the Norman Conquest, the two countries were at peace in the 13th century. But peace ended with the Scottish succession debate (the Great Cause) following the death of King Alexander III in 1286.

Initially, King Edward I of England managed to impose English rule on Scotland. But in 1306, Robert the Bruce rebelled and claimed the Scottish crown, setting off another stage in the Wars of Independence that began in 1296.

After Edward I's death in 1307, Bruce enjoyed 20 years of military success against the new English king, Edward II. Bruce is especially well-known for his victory at Bannockburn in 1314.

By 1327, Edward II had been forced to give up his crown due to a rebellion led by his wife, Queen Isabella, and a majority of the nobles, who had long disliked his weak rule.

Queen Isabella and the English Parliament were prepared to make peace on Bruce's terms. In return, the

Scottish would pay war reparations of £20,000, a vast amount at that time. Bruce would finally be recognized by the English as king of an independent Scotland.

The promises were all laid out in a treaty, which was ratified in Edinburgh in March 1328 and by the English Parliament at Northampton in May. The treaty was sealed by the marriage of Joan, the sister of Edward III, to Bruce's heir, David.

Known in England as the "Shameful Peace" because it surrendered long-claimed English rights, the treaty did not last long. In 1333, Edward III invaded Scotland, and the Wars of Independence began again, lasting off and on for nearly 300 years.

—PROFESSOR CHRISTOPHER GIVEN-WILSON

PART III: 1346–1485

BATTLE OF CRÉCY

1346

During the 14th and 15th centuries, England was not only at war with Scotland but also engaged in a long dispute with France.

This lengthy on-again off-again conflict between England and France is called the Hundred Years' War (1337–1453). King Edward III began the war in 1337, just four years after breaking peace with Scotland.

Edward's goals were to maintain his control over English-held territories in France, defend and expand English economic interests on the Continent, and press a claim to the French throne.

In the summer of 1346, he led an invasion force across northern France to harass and pillage enemy territories and capture important towns. Although his expedition had much success, its progress was halted in late August near the village of Crécy by a much larger French army.

The resulting Battle of Crécy, fought on August 26, was one of the most famous of the war. Though greatly outnumbered, Edward demonstrated tactical and technological superiority over his opponents. Having chosen the high ground, he carefully

organized his soldiers into defensive formations and prepared a system of ditches, pits, and obstacles for the enemy cavalry.

Perhaps overconfident in their greater numbers, the French army hastily and foolishly launched several advances of crossbowmen and cavalry. Edward's extensive use of the longbow devastated the attacking French units, which were unable to break the disciplined English line. The English won a decisive victory with minor loss of life on their side.

Edward's unexpected victory at Crécy threw the French into disarray. This battle set the tone for a long period of English military success during the 1350s and 1360s.

—DR. GILBERT BOGNER

GEOFFREY CHAUCER

1343-1400

Geoffrey Chaucer, the father of English literature, came from a family of rich wine merchants. As a teenager he joined King Edward III's army. He was captured during an invasion of France but was soon freed, thanks to the king. By 1367, he had entered royal service under the patronage of the king's son John of Gaunt. Later he would even become a member of Parliament.

Although he held many jobs during his life, Chaucer is best remembered for his poetry. *The Book of the Duchess*, his first major poem, was written in memory of John of Gaunt's first wife, Blanche of Lancaster.

Chaucer's most famous poem is *The Canterbury Tales*. This work follows the journey of a group of fictional pilgrims traveling from Southwark to Canterbury. Its characters include a friar, a knight, and a cook. Their stories are told vividly, giving us a real insight into the lives of medieval people, both rich and poor.

—HARRIET HOWES

THE BLACK DEATH

1348-1350

The Black Death was the greatest natural disaster in European history, killing 50 percent or more of the continent's population in just three years. The disease was probably bubonic plague (the bacillus *Yersinia pestis*), spread by the flea *Xenopsylla cheopsis* carried by black rats.

The Black Death reached Europe from Asia in late 1347. The plague spread northward through France and Germany, and it arrived on the south coast of England in the summer of 1348 (although in many parts of England, the most devastation occurred in 1349).

English manorial and church records provide details of the impact of the disease. From these records, historians know that many towns and villages lost half or more of their population—and some were wiped out entirely.

By 1350, the disease had moved on to other parts of Europe, but the legacy of the catastrophe lasted for centuries. Before 1347, Europe had a labor surplus, resulting in high rents and prices and low wages. But the Black Death reversed these trends. Those who survived enjoyed a period of better living standards called the "Golden Age of the Peasantry."

But the disease would appear again. Regular outbreaks devastated the populace throughout the 15th and 16th centuries.

Not until about 1750 did England's population recover to its 1347 level of six or seven million.

—PROFESSOR CHRISTOPHER GIVEN-WILSON

ANNE OF BOHEMIA

1366-1394

Anne of Bohemia, the daughter of a Holy Roman Emperor, became the Queen Consort of England as the wife of King Richard II.

Their marriage was controversial. One mean-spirited English chronicler even called Anne a "tiny scrap of humanity" because he thought Richard should have married a more prestigious woman with a larger dowry. Yet Richard and Anne, both only 15 years old when they married, truly loved each other.

She was a peacemaker, softening her husband's heart toward wrongdoers and enemies. Londoners were so grateful to her for mending a quarrel between them and the king that they gave her a live pelican, a rare bird and a symbol of Anne's piety.

Due to her kind nature and her reform Christian upbringing, she's also said to have protected John Wycliffe and the Lollards who followed him. Wycliffe translated the Bible from Latin into English and challenged the authority of religious leaders.

She was also an inspiration to Chaucer, who based a character on her and wrote a book at her request.

Yet she and Richard failed at the most important task of any royal couple, to produce heirs (preferably male ones, at that).

When Anne died of the plague 12 years after their marriage, Richard was so miserable that he demolished the palace at Sheen where she had breathed her last breath. Anne of Bohemia has been long remembered by the English as their own beloved Good Queen Anne.

—GREYSON BEIGHTS

MARGERY KEMPE

1373-1438

Margery Kempe wrote the first autobiography in the English language. She was born in 1373 to a prosperous family in the port of Lynn, where her father was mayor.

When Margery grew up, she married John Kempe, and they had 14 children. Although she worked as a brewer and a miller, both businesses failed. This was an ordinary life for a woman around 1400, but other parts of Margery's life were truly extraordinary.

Margery was a Christian mystic and believed that Jesus spoke to her directly. As a sign of her holiness, she wanted to wear white clothes, and the archbishop of Canterbury gave her permission to do so. She also tried to convince everyone—husband, neighbors, priests, bishops—that she could perform miracles.

Sometimes Margery succeeded in persuading them, but other times she didn't. Some thought she was a fraud. Because she screamed and cried loudly whenever she had a vision, even her supporters sometimes found her tiresome.

Margery was an enthusiastic pilgrim. She traveled to holy places like Rome, Jerusalem, Santiago de Compostela, and many other shrines. Although Margery could not read, she had an exceptional memory and could recite passages from books that had been read to her. Just before she died, she dictated her life story to a scribe.

Now known as *The Book of Margery Kempe*, her autobiography tells a fascinating story about urban life, pilgrimage, and faith in late medieval England.

—GREYSON BEIGHTS

PEASANTS' REVOLT

1381

The Peasants' Revolt of 1381 is the most famous uprising of the Middle Ages in England. The Black Death had turned a labor surplus into a labor shortage, driving wages up and rents down. Landowners, who dominated Parliament, reacted by passing labor laws to force wages down, which greatly upset the peasants.

The 1370s also saw English military failure, political scandal, and high taxation.

A poll tax was the spark that ignited the rebellion, causing riots in Kent and Essex against tax collectors. This poll tax, or head tax, had to be paid to the king by every adult except the very poorest, at the rate of 12 pence per person.

Led by Wat Tyler and the priest John Ball, the rebels marched on London and occupied the city for three days (June 13 through June 15). They burned, looted, and killed hundreds of lawyers, foreigners, and royal officials, including the chancellor and the treasurer. Meanwhile, the young King Richard II hid in the Tower of London.

The rebels met twice with the king, who promised to free them from serfdom and reform the government. But after the rebels left London, these promises were broken and hundreds were tried and executed.

Unrest had also broken out in many other parts of the country. Conflict continued until late July, by which time the government had recovered

FIGHTING IN THE STREETS

its nerve. Although it seemed as if the revolt achieved little, serfdom rapidly disappeared from England after 1381. The government, wary of inciting another revolt, did away with the hated poll taxes.

—PROFESSOR CHRISTOPHER GIVEN-WILSON

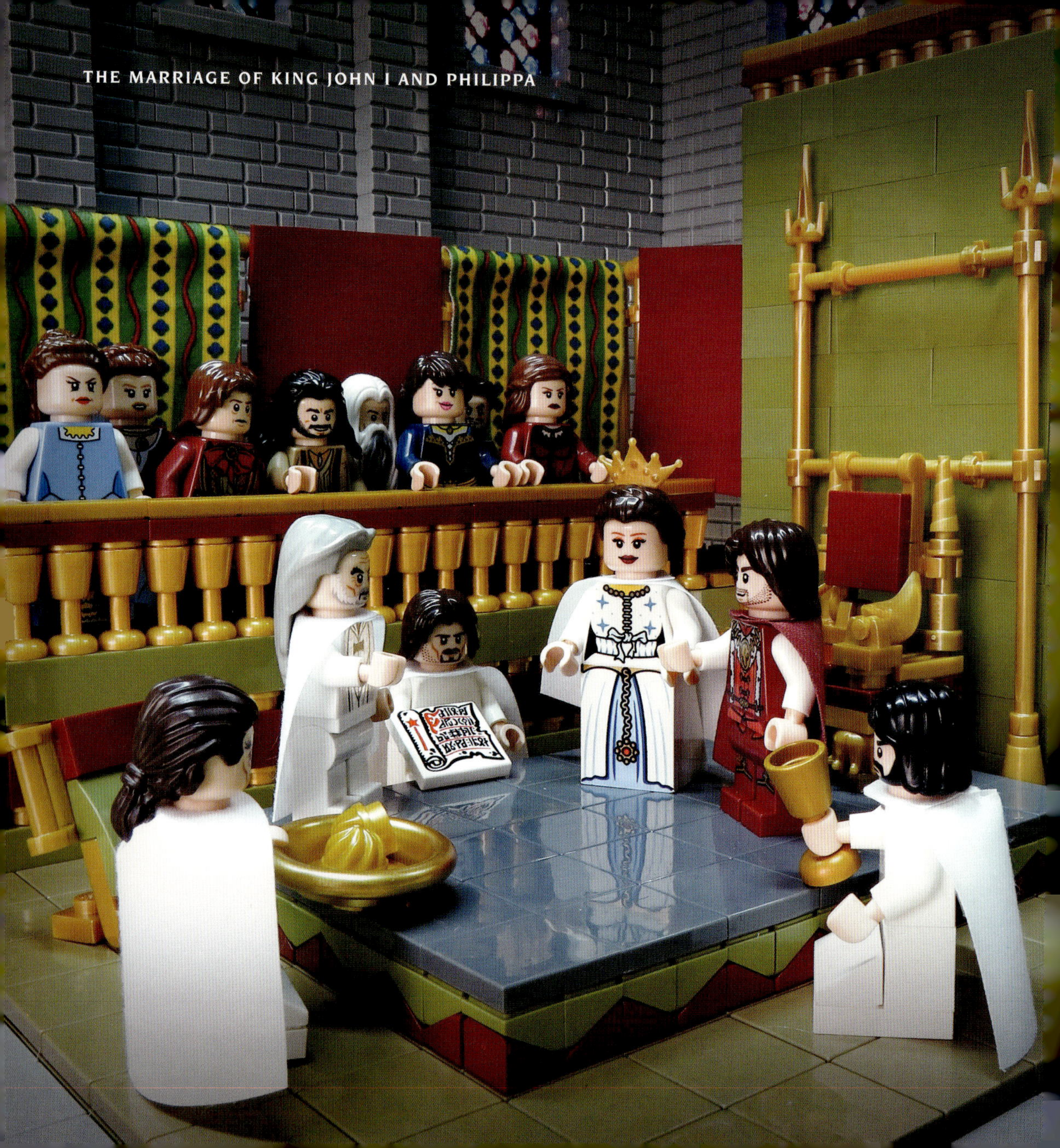

THE MARRIAGE OF KING JOHN I AND PHILIPPA

TREATY OF WINDSOR

1386

Although the Hundred Years' War (1337–1453) was fought between England and France, several other kingdoms were drawn into the conflict. These smaller kingdoms included Castile, a kingdom in Spain that allied with France, and Portugal, which allied with England.

The Treaty of Windsor was made between England and Portugal on May 9, 1386. It was sealed by the marriage of King John I of Portugal to Philippa, the daughter of John of Gaunt, Duke of Lancaster.

John of Gaunt claimed the throne of Castile through his wife and hoped that the Portuguese king would help him secure it. But instead, Gaunt gave up his claim to Castile in 1387 in return for a large cash settlement.

The English-Portuguese treaty has remained in force ever since and is the oldest diplomatic alliance in the world. It has been sorely tested at times, especially during the 17th-century Dutch-Portuguese War and the 19th-century colonial wars of conquest in Africa.

The marriage between King John I and Philippa was also a great success. Their children, known in Portuguese history as the Illustrious Generation, included Henry the Navigator, a great explorer.

—PROFESSOR CHRISTOPHER GIVEN-WILSON

BATTLE OF AGINCOURT

1415

Following a decades-long period of truce, the Hundred Years' War was renewed in 1415 by King Henry V of England.

Reviving demands for lands in France, he also reasserted a claim to the French throne made by his great-grandfather Edward III at the beginning of the war. Henry brought an army across the English Channel in August 1415.

After losing many of his men to disease during the long siege of Harfleur on the north coast of France, the king led his army across Normandy.

Weakened, ill, and exhausted, the army was blocked by a much greater French force near the village of Agincourt. The result was one of the most celebrated battles in English history. On the morning of October 25, Henry positioned his army on a strip of land between two wooded areas, hoping to reduce the effectiveness of the superior French numbers. Then, taking a bold risk, Henry advanced his army to a second position. Within longbow range of the French, his archers began firing.

The overconfident French men-at-arms responded by charging across the wet, freshly plowed field. Slogging through the mud under a hail of arrows, the men in the front line were pushed and trampled by their fellow soldiers from behind. Most fell before even reaching the English line. Thousands of French were killed or captured, prompting the remainder to flee the field.

THE ENGLISH LINE

This remarkable victory led to a second campaign in which Henry subdued much of northern France by 1420, the high point of English success in the war. Following King Henry V's death in 1422, the French slowly regained the advantage and eventually drove the English out of France in 1453.

—DR. GILBERT BOGNER

FIRST BATTLE OF ST ALBANS

1455

On May 22, 1455, as King Henry VI of Lancaster traveled from London to Leicester, his retinue was attacked in the town of St Albans by the retinues of Richard, Duke of York, and his allies, the Earls of Salisbury and Warwick. Richard had a claim to the throne, and some people thought he would be a better king than Henry.

Henry had about 2,000 men with him, and the Yorkists had about 3,000.

A skirmish, rather than a pitched battle, took place in the town's streets. Although the fight lasted just a few hours, the encounter is considered the beginning of the Wars of the Roses. The white rose was the emblem of the Duke of York and the red rose became an emblem of the House of Lancaster.

King Henry VI was wounded in the neck and captured by the Duke of York. Henry's kinsman and chief minister, the Duke of Somerset, and several other nobles were killed. The Duke of York took charge of the kingdom and controlled the king's government for a time.

This bloodshed created new family feuds among the nobility and deepened the dynastic hostility between Lancaster and York. The First Battle of St Albans began a period of many fierce battles pitting King Henry VI against Richard, Duke of York.

—PROFESSOR RALPH GRIFFITHS

BATTLE OF TOWTON

1461

The Duke of York's victory at the First Battle of St Albans gave him a short-term grip on power. But his success brought a more deadly foe to the fore in Henry VI's queen, Margaret of Anjou.

In 1459, full-scale civil war erupted between the Houses of Lancaster and York. Seven battles of increasing ferocity took place between the two armies, culminating in Towton in March 1461. Fought in the most appalling conditions of sleet and snow, it was the bloodiest battle ever fought on English soil.

The Battle of Towton ended as a decisive Yorkist victory. The Duke of York had been killed three months before, but his son was now crowned as Edward IV.

—GEORGE GOODWIN

FOOTMEN RUNNING FROM THE CAVALRY

BATTLE OF BOSWORTH FIELD

1485

In 1483, few expected that the young Henry Tudor would become king of England by 1485. His connection with England's royal family was distant, and he had no training as a future king. Because he was a Lancastrian and a York king was in power, he lived for many years in the northwest of modern France, in Brittany.

For decades, the Houses of Lancaster (the red rose) and York (the white rose) had fought over the throne. In 1483, it was held by King Richard III of the House of York, who was hated by many. So Henry Tudor took his chances and led the Lancastrians in a rebellion against Richard.

On August 7, 1485, with the French king's aid, Henry landed in Milford Sound in southwest Wales. As he marched through Wales to the English midlands, he attracted support, in part because of his Welsh ancestry. Then near Market Bosworth, a town west of Leicester, Thomas Stanley, Earl of Derby, provided crucial forces.

The battle of Bosworth Field on August 22, 1485, was the last decisive battle of the Wars of the Roses. After only a few hours, Henry's English, French, and Welsh soldiers, reinforced by artillery, defeated Richard's much larger army. They triumphed when Richard charged Henry's lines and was slain.

Richard's body was buried in the Franciscan friary in Leicester, now long gone. In 2012, a skeleton was discovered beneath a parking garage. The evidence suggests that it is King Richard's, and he has been reburied in Leicester Cathedral.

The Yorkist dynasty of English kings—the shortest in English history—ended with the death of King Richard III. The victorious Henry Tudor became King Henry VII, and his direct descendants ruled England until 1603. Henry would be the last English king to attain the throne through battle.

The Battle of Bosworth Field is considered by some to mark the end of the Middle Ages in England. It helped to restore political stability, marking the end of a truly fascinating era.

—PROFESSOR RALPH GRIFFITHS

• SCHOLARS •

PROFESSOR PHILLIP C. ADAMO is Associate Professor of History and Director of Medieval Studies at Augsburg College in Minneapolis. He has published articles and books on medieval monasticism and church history. He is also an award-winning teacher, most recently the recipient of the CARA Award for Excellence in Teaching, given by the Medieval Academy of America, the oldest and largest association of medievalists in the world. *Battle of Falkirk*

PROFESSOR JOHN ARNOLD is Professor of Medieval History at Birkbeck, University of London and has held that position since 2008. He has worked at Birkbeck, University of London since 2001, and before that was a lecturer at the University of East Anglia. He primarily works on aspects of medieval religious culture but has also published on issues in historiography and public history. *Roger Bacon, William Wallace, and The Great Famine*

PROFESSOR ROBERT BARTLETT, FBA, FRSE, is Bishop Wardlaw Professor of Mediaeval History at the University of St Andrews, Scotland, and a Fellow of the British Academy. His publications include *The Making of Europe: Conquest, Colonization and Cultural Change* 950–1350 (Princeton University Press, 1993), which won the Wolfson History Prize; *England under the Norman and Angevin Kings* 1075–1225 (Oxford University Press, 2000); and *Why Can the Dead Do Such Great Things?: Saints and Worshippers from the Martyrs to the Reformation* (Princeton University Press, 2013). He has presented three television series for the BBC. *Death of William Rufus, The Captivity of Richard the Lionheart, The Founding of the University of Oxford, and Treaty of York*

DR. GILBERT BOGNER teaches medieval history at Saint Vincent College in Latrobe, Pennsylvania, where he has been a member of the faculty for sixteen years. He earned his PhD in 1997 from Ohio University, where he met and married his lovely wife, Elyse. Dr. Bogner's research interests lie in 15th-century English knighthood, about which he has published several articles. His hobbies include toy collecting and reading comic books. His son, Harry, loves all things LEGO. *William the Conqueror, Battle of Crécy, and Battle of Agincourt*

PROFESSOR D'ARCY JONATHAN DACRE BOULTON was born in Toronto, Canada, in 1946, and educated at the University of Toronto (Honors BA, 1969); the University of Pennsylvania (PhD in medieval studies, 1978); and the University of Oxford, England (DPhil in medieval history, 1976). He has taught at Davidson College, Harvard University, and, since 1985, the University of Notre Dame, where he is a Professor of Medieval Studies and History. His field of specialization is the nobilities of France and England. *First English Prince of Wales*

PROFESSOR DAVID D'AVRAY is a medievalist who has worked on medieval marriage, preaching, attitudes to kingship and death, and rationalities. He has written countless publications on medieval topics. His most recent book is *Dissolving Royal Marriages: A Documentary History*, 860–1600 (Cambridge University Press, 2014). He is Professor of History at University College London and a Fellow of the British Academy. *Eleanor of Aquitaine*

PROFESSOR JOHN FRANCE is a medievalist and a longtime member of the History Department at Swansea University in the United Kingdom who served as Visiting Professor at West Point. His specialties are warfare and crusading, on which he has published extensively. His latest book is *Perilous Glory: Understanding Western Warfare* (Yale University Press, 2011), a history of war from the earliest times to the present day. *Siege of Jerusalem and Siege of Acre*

PROFESSOR CHRISTOPHER GIVEN-WILSON is Professor Emeritus of Medieval History at the University of St Andrews, Scotland. He is the author or editor of nine books and around thirty articles on 14th- and 15th-century British history, and general editor of *The Parliament Rolls of Medieval England* 1275–1504 (Scholarly Digital Editions, 2005). He specializes in the political and social history of the Late Middle Ages. At St Andrews he teaches advanced-level courses on the Peasants' Revolt, the Hundred Years' War, and Inca Civilization. *Treaty of Edinburgh-Northampton, The Black Death, Peasants' Revolt, and Treaty of Windsor*

GEORGE GOODWIN is the author of *Fatal Colours: Towton 1461 - England's Bloodiest Battle* and of *Fatal Rivalry: Henry VIII, James IV and the Battle for Renaissance Britain* (both published by W.W. Norton). He is a graduate of Cambridge University and a Fellow of the Royal Society of Arts and the Chartered Institute of Marketing. His next book, *Benjamin Franklin in London: The British Life of America's Founding Father*, will be published in 2016. (georgegoodwin.com) *Battle of Towton*

PROFESSOR RALPH GRIFFITHS was formerly Professor of Medieval History at Swansea University, United Kingdom. His main fields of research and writing are political and social history of the British Isles from the 13th to the 16th century. His books include *The Principality of Wales in the Later Middle Ages* (University of Wales Press, 1972), *The Reign of King Henry VI* (The History Press, 2005), *The Oxford Illustrated History of the British Monarchy* (Oxford University Press, 1998), and *The Making of the Tudor Dynasty* (The History Press, 2005). *First Battle of St Albans and Battle of Bosworth Field*

HARRIET HOWES is a PhD candidate at Queen Mary University of London. She received her BA in English Literature from Cambridge University in 2011 and her MPhil in Medieval Literature from the same institution in 2012. She is researching late medieval devotional prose texts. Her work focuses on recurring tropes of water, frequently implemented in these texts to allegorize and explore spiritual Christian life. *Geoffrey Chaucer*

DR. STEVEN ISAAC teaches at Longwood University in Virginia. He has published chapters and articles on medieval military history in books, encyclopedias, *Journal of Medieval Military History*, and *Les Cahiers de Civilisation Médiévale*. His current projects are threefold: the role of mercenaries, the impact of being besieged on urban populations, and the War of 1173–74. He manages the Haskins Society website (*http://www.haskinssociety.org/*). In addition, he co-organizes a student research conference at Longwood (*http://www.longwood.edu/medieval/*). *Battle of the Standard*

PROFESSOR STEPHEN KNIGHT is a Research Professor in English Literature at the University of Melbourne, Australia. A graduate of Oxford and Sydney, he has worked at universities in Australia, England, and Wales and has written widely on medieval and modern literature, specializing in crime fiction (*The Mysteries of the Cities*, McFarland, 2012) and Robin Hood (*Reading Robin Hood: Content, Form and Reception*, Manchester University Press, forthcoming). *Robin Hood*

DR. ANNE LAWRENCE-MATHERS is Associate Professor in Medieval History at the University of Reading, where she teaches on medieval culture and society, and especially on medieval magic. She studied Anglo-Saxon, Norse, and Celtic at Cambridge before doing a PhD on English monastic manuscripts at the Courtauld Institute of Art (London). Anne has published books and articles on manuscripts in Northumbria, Merlin the Magician, medieval magical texts, women and education, and history-writing in medieval England. *Matthew Paris*

DR. STEPHEN MORILLO (Harvard AB, Oxford DPhil) specializes in world history, medieval history, and military history, combining the three in various ways in his teaching and research. He is the author of a number of books and articles on these topics, most recently *Frameworks of World History* (Oxford University Press, 2013), a world history textbook. He teaches at Wabash College in Indiana, and is currently working on a graphic history book with his wife, Lynne Miles. *Battle of Hastings*

DR. KATHLEEN NEAL teaches history at the Centre for Medieval and Renaissance Studies at Monash University in Melbourne, Australia. She does research on the history of England in the 13th century, especially political events and how they influenced people's lives. Interestingly, she has been fascinated by Magna Carta since she was eight years old. Every day, she can't believe how lucky she is to have a job as a historian and think about the medieval world all day. *Excommunication of King John, Signing of Magna Carta, and First English Parliament*

The author would like to thank **PROFESSOR JUDITH M. BENNETT** of the University of Southern California for her help with the *Anne of Bohemia* and *Margery Kempe* entries.

• BUILDERS •

Photographs provided by the builders of their respective models. All copyrights retained by the individual copyright holders. Additional photographs and models by the author.

MICHAEL AND NATHAN FEIST are brothers who grew up in Briarcliff Manor, New York. Michael is a college student whose interests include history, Latin, photography, astronomy, and linguistics. Nathan is studying food science at Cornell University. His interests include television, films, music, and languages. *Battle of Crécy (p. 82)*

ELLIOTT FELDMAN is an AFOL (adult fan of LEGO) from Bakersfield, California. His hobbies include music composition, filmmaking, and soccer. *Battle of Hastings (p. 6, 9) and Treaty of Edinburgh-Northampton (p. 76)*

CARSON HART is a LEGO builder from Hermosa Beach, California. His hobbies include building, drawing, photography, surfing, skateboarding, baseball, and volleyball. His work has also been featured in *Beautiful* LEGO (No Starch Press, 2013), and he's acted as curator for ReBrick, the LEGO Group's official fan blog. *Geoffrey Chaucer (p. 88)*

BEN HAUGER has been building original historical LEGO creations, including pirate ships and castles, for many years. He is an active member of TwinLUG, a Guild Leader of Eurobrick.com's Guilds of Historica, and the History Moderator of Eurobricks.com. When not injuring his thumbs pressing together ABS bricks, he enjoys family time with his wife, Rachel, and their son, Miles. *The Captivity of Richard the Lionheart (p.28) and Peasants' Revolt (p. 98, 101)*

PAUL HETHERINGTON is an award-winning LEGO artist based in Vancouver, Canada. He started building with LEGO again at age 21 and has been building and collecting LEGO ever since. Over the past 15 years, Paul has made many large, detailed LEGO models that represent a wide range of themes. *Treaty of Windsor (p. 102)*

RYAN HOWERTER is a student of graphic design. He has built with LEGO for most of his life. Apart from LEGO, Ryan likes music, vegan food, and making things. His recent LEGO projects include commissioned NASA-inspired builds and a definitive reference of all LEGO colors. *Treaty of York (p. 57) and The Black Death (p. 90)*

LUKA KAMBIČ was born in Radovljica, a small town in Slovenia. He loves to build with LEGO bricks and started at an early age playing with his brother with just a few small sets. *First English Parliament (p. 58)*

JONAS KLEINALSTEDE is a LEGO builder from Cloppenburg, Germany. Some of his hobbies include drawing, photography, and music. *Excommunication of King John (p. 32)*

GÜNTHER MÖBIUS is a LEGO builder from Berlin, Germany. He is an avid amateur photographer, artist, and percussionist. His work has also been featured in *Beautiful* LEGO 2: *Dark* (No Starch Press, 2014). *Siege of Jerusalem (p. 10), Eleanor of Aquitaine (p. 18), Matthew Paris (p. 46–47, 49), Anne of Bohemia (p. 92), and First Battle of St Albans (p. 110–111, 112)*

JAMES PEGRUM is a fan of history and LEGO from the United Kingdom. He has been combining his two interests for a number of years, charting the history of his country in highly detailed historical LEGO scenes. He is a founding member of Bricks to the Past, a group that researches and builds large collaborative historical displays. *Siege of Acre (p. 24)*

HENRIK PERSSON is a LEGO enthusiast from Sweden. He rediscovered his love for LEGO as an adult, and after that all other hobbies were quickly abandoned. He enjoys building fantasy- and medieval-themed creations but also dabbles in other genres. He is an active member of the Swedish LEGO community, Swebrick. *William the Conqueror (p. 2), Death of William Rufus (p. 14), Signing of Magna Carta (p. 42), and Battle of Towton (p. 115)*

KYLE RANSOM is a LEGO artist, athlete, and high school student from Logan, Utah. He has been building with LEGO for as long as he can remember, and he began using it as an art medium in 2012 after discovering the online LEGO community. His other hobbies include mountain biking, skiing, running, and reading. *Death of William Rufus (p. 17), William Wallace (p. 64), and The Great Famine (p. 74)*

ISAAC SNYDER is an active LEGO builder who is well-known on Eurobricks, Classic-Castle.com, and MOCPages. He enjoys reading about medieval history and is often inspired to create new models based on what he's read. All of his creations can be seen at brickbuilt.org, through which you can also commission custom builds or copies of Isaac's models. *William Wallace (p. 62) and Battle of Falkirk (p. 66, 68)*

PAUL VERMEESCH is a student, creative, and entrepreneur. Chesterton and Kuyper are found on his bookshelves, and he'll happily strike up a conversation about art, theology, music, or horses over a cup of Earl Grey. He lives on a farm in Northern Michigan and is studying at Wheaton College in Illinois. *First English Prince of Wales (p. 70)*

• THE AUTHOR •

GREYSON BEIGHTS is a third-year university student and award-winning LEGO builder. He also helps organize BrickUniverse, a LEGO convention for fans of all ages that is held annually in Raleigh, North Carolina, and Dallas, Texas.